MAWSON
Antarctic Explorer

R.T. Watts

1

KNOWLEDGE
BOOKS AND SOFTWARE

Teacher Notes:

This chapter book focusses on the science of Antarctica as well as the great achievements of Sir Douglas Mawson. The focus is fluency with reading with a sustainability perspective in relation to Antarctica as a conservation case study.

Discussion points for consideration:

1. Douglas Mawson was successful in exploring Antarctica. Why did he do this? Look at goal-setting and team-building.

2. Antarctica is owned by nobody. How are countries managing to share Antarctica? Do you think Antarctica should be mined?

3. How did Douglas Mawson get to explore Antarctica? What did he have to do to get there? Research how he got the money and support.

4. You want to explore the unexplored mountains of Papua New Guinea. Make a pitch using Microsoft® Powerpoint.

Difficult words to be introduced and practised before reading this book:

Antarctica, geology, expedition, university, Adelaide, continent, Australia, America, Mawson, happened, exploring, important, disappearing, algae, horizon, chocolate, everyone, beautiful, aurora, radiation, cyclone, weather, temperature, glaciers, linseed, Commonwealth, donor, crevasse, poison, kilometres, rescue, information, understanding.

Contents

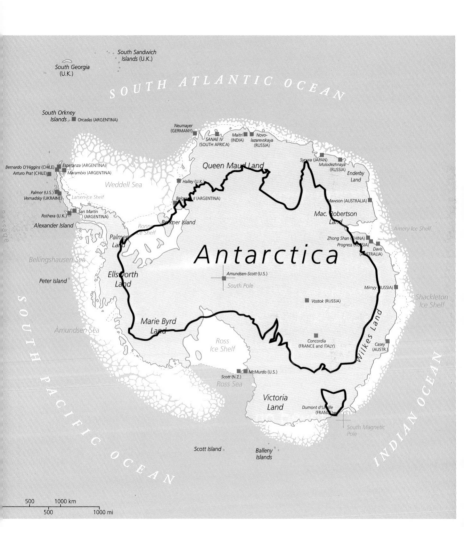

South Sandwich
Islands (U.K.)

South Georgia
(U.K.)

SOUTH ATLANTIC OCEAN

South Orkney
Islands ▪ Orcadas (ARGENTINA)

Neumayer
(GERMANY)
SANAE IV
(SOUTH AFRICA)
Maitri
(INDIA)
Novo-
lazarevskaya
(RUSSIA)

Queen Maud Land

Syowa (JAPAN)

Bernardo O'Higgins (CHILE) ▪ Esperanza (ARGENTINA)
Arturo Prat (CHILE) ▪ ▪ Marambio (ARGENTINA)

Molodezhnaya
(RUSSIA)
Enderby
Land

Weddell Sea

Halley (U.K.)

Palmer (U.S.)
Vernadsky (UKRAINE)

Belgrano II (ARGENTINA)

Larsen Ice Shelf

Mac. Robertson
Land

Mawson (AUSTRALIA)

Rothera (U.K.)
San Martin
(ARGENTINA)

Berkner Island

Alexander Island

Palmer
Land

Ronne
Ice Shelf

Amery Ice Shelf

Zhong Shan (CHINA)
Progress (RUSSIA)

Bellingshausen Sea

Ellsworth
Land

Antarctica

Davis
(AUSTRALIA)

Peter Island

Amundsen-Scott (U.S.)
South Pole

Mirny (RUSSIA)

Shackleton
Ice Shelf

Vostok (RUSSIA)

Amundsen Sea

Marie Byrd
Land

Ross
Ice Shelf

Concordia
(FRANCE and ITALY)

Casey
(AUSTR.)

Wilkes Land

SOUTH PACIFIC OCEAN

McMurdo (U.S.)

Scott (N.Z.)
Ross Sea

Victoria
Land

Dumont d'Urville
(FRANCE)

INDIAN OCEAN

South Magnetic
Pole

Scott Island

Balleny
Islands

500   1000 km

500   1000 mi

1

1. About the Ice Man

Douglas Mawson was born in England but came to Australia as a two-year-old. He grew up in Sydney and went to university and studied engineering. Mawson went to the Pacific islands and looked at the geology. This was followed by more geology work, after which he began teaching geology at the University of Adelaide.

Mawson joined an expedition to Antarctica in 1907 to 1909. They climbed Antarctica's highest mountain and went inland to the South Pole. They stayed on during the winter and continued with the study of Antarctica's weather and geology. Mawson was asked to join other groups to explore Antarctica.

2. Antarctica: The Frozen Continent

The interest in Antarctica goes back before Captain James Cook explored the Pacific and Eastern Australia. Cook was told to look for the "Great South Land". The British already knew about Australia and called it "New Holland". The British wanted to find the "Great South Land" as they thought it would be a huge, rich place which could be the new America.

Cook went back to the Pacific to explore south again. This time he went south as far as he could go. He sailed south until he could not move from the ice packs. He was very close to Antarctica. Cook had run into a wall of ice and had to turn back.

This time he knew it was time to turn back. When he got back to England, he said it was a frozen land of winds and snow. He had not found the "Great South Land". They stopped exploring south of Australia.

The British then decided to make Australia a colony of Britain. This began with the colony in New South Wales.

Antarctica was visited by whalers and sealers. These boats went south looking for seals for fur and whales for oil. The whalers came from Britain and America.

Whaling was important as it gave them whale oil. Whale oil was used for lighting and as an oil for machines. It was a very good oil.

Antarctica is full of animal life. All the food for the animals comes from the cold waters. It starts with tiny critters and plants. These sea critters are food for fish and animals. As the animals get larger, so do their food needs. This is called the food chain.

Whales eat a lot of these tiny critters for food. They need tons of these little critters. The seals eat small fish. The seals are then food for orcas or sharks. And so the food chain of animals and plants starts in the cold waters around Antarctica.

Why are the Antarctic waters making so much food? The reason is that the cold water is rich in minerals and carbon dioxide which makes algae grow very fast.

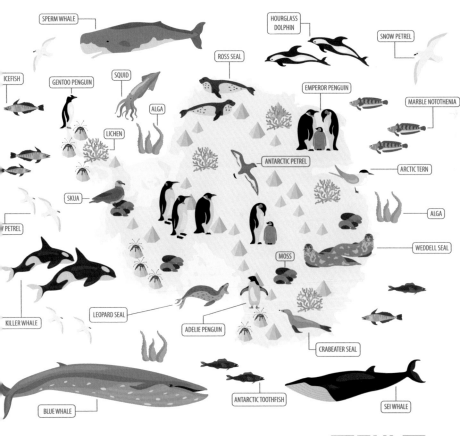

SPERM WHALE

HOURGLASS DOLPHIN

SNOW PETREL

ICEFISH

GENTOO PENGUIN

SQUID

ROSS SEAL

EMPEROR PENGUIN

ALGA

LICHEN

MARBLE NOTOTHENIA

ANTARCTIC PETREL

ARCTIC TERN

SKUA

ALGA

PETREL

WEDDELL SEAL

MOSS

KILLER WHALE

LEOPARD SEAL

ADELIE PENGUIN

CRABEATER SEAL

BLUE WHALE

ANTARCTIC TOOTHFISH

SEI WHALE

9

Antarctica is a frozen continent. It is very cold and is covered in ice all year. In winter, the Sun never rises above the horizon. The winter is dark all the time. It is a very difficult place to stay in winter. You need to be a special and very calm person. If you get cranky, you will be fighting over many things. Some people have fought over a chocolate bar.

In summer, the Sun never goes down. It goes slowly toward the horizon and then rises again at one o'clock in the morning. It can be very hard to sleep. Some people do not like the summer as it stops them from sleeping.

The land and sky are beautiful and special. The night has the Aurora Australis lights. These are the lights of the Sun's radiation hitting the air.

The winds in Antarctica are very strong. It is like living in a cyclone all year. The winds are so strong that they will blow you over when trying to walk. There are some calm days but not many.

The weather in Antarctica controls a lot of the world's weather. It controls Australia's weather. If you want to know when we will get rain, drought, storms and calm weather, then it is Antarctica's weather which is the key.

The climate in Antarctica is dry and very cold. In summer, the temperature on any day is -40 degrees Celsius. This is cold enough to freeze your skin quickly.

It is also a very dry place. It is the driest place on Earth.

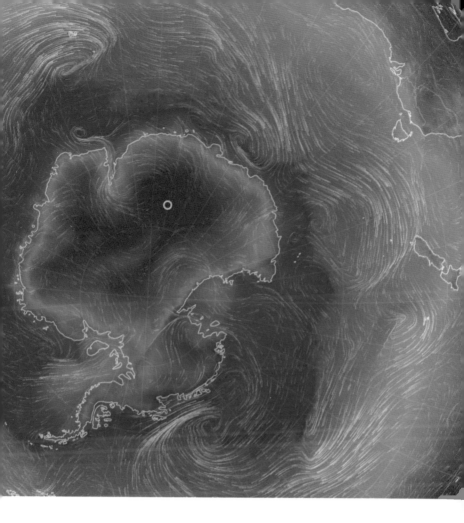

3. Gear and Supplies Needed

Why did Mawson go to Antarctica? In winter, it is night all the time. And in summer, it is day all the time.

After his first trip with another group he wanted to have his own expedition. This was a trip to study the plant and animal life, the rocks and earth, the weather and the seas. He was a great scientist as well as an explorer. He had to be very mentally tough, strong and fit to be able to do what he did.

Mawson travelled along the coast of Antarctica. He went over 1000km along the coast and then returned. This was across glaciers and through very bad weather. Antarctica is a massive place which is bigger than Australia.

They had to wear special clothes. The jackets and pants were a double knot cotton covered in linseed oil. They were worn loose so the sweat could get out. If the sweat gets to the air it will freeze to your skin.

The gloves were wolf fur as these were the warmest. These were mittens with rope tying these together in case they fell off your hands. Your hands would have little time before freezing if left out in the cold.

The oil coating stopped the wind and ice getting through to the skin. Underneath the coat were wool liners to protect the body. The boots had to have very thick soles. The thick sole and inside liners were reeds. The soles of the boots had ice-spikes called crampons.

17

The sled was made of special wood. It was a strong wood which could carry a load of goods for the trip.

The sled was pulled by dogs. These dogs were big dogs from the Arctic called huskies. They were tied together using a series of leads so the dogs could walk at the same pace.

The dogs had to have a lot of food to keep strong. This food had to be towed as well.

Food had to be brought from Australia and the UK. They brought a lot of food and coal.

The food had to be stored in the hut to stop animals breaking the cans and bottles. They also lived in the hut while they were waiting for the ship to return.

Everything was stored in Mawson's hut. The snow built up around the hut and sometimes they had to climb in and out via the roof.

The sled dogs were big. They were a dog that came from the Arctic area such as Greenland. The dogs Mawson used were from Tasmania, Macquarie and Heard Islands, and Greenland.

The dogs were kept and bred for the local conditions. They were tough and strong and could pull sleds and work all day. The dogs had to survive in icy conditions and wake up ready to keep working. They ate seal meat, blubber, beef pieces and fat. The fat makes energy to stay warm in the snow.

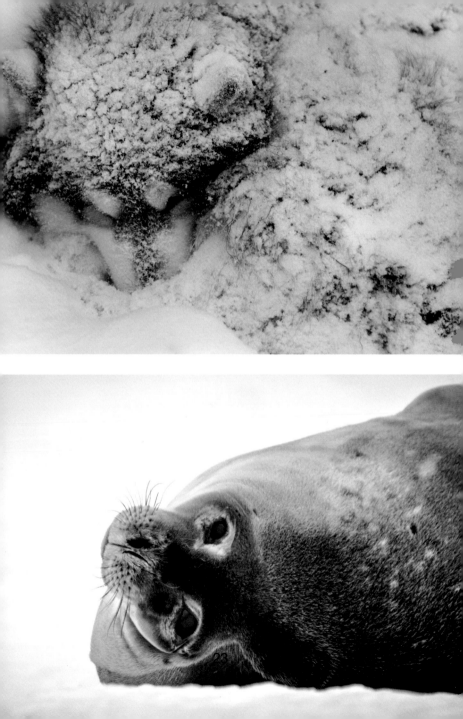

4. Setting Up Base

They set up their base at Commonwealth Bay, which is now called Mawson. Their ship brought all the food, equipment and fuel.

A hut was built to hold all the supplies. This had to be strong enough to last a long time. The cabin had to last over the winter and summer. To keep warm, they needed fuel for heating. Today there are still tins, bottles and tools left in Mawson's hut. These have been there for over 100 years.

The amount of money needed for all the stuff was tremendous. This money came from a rich person and other people in Australia and Britain.

25

Commonwealth Bay was one of the windiest parts of Antarctica. The winds blew twice as strong as other areas. Mawson had chosen a wrong place for a base.

The strong winds in Antarctica are caused by the winds rushing down from the mountains. The air is super cold and can be - 60 degrees Celsius. The air is so cold that your skin will freeze in seconds. The mountains make the strong winds blowing across Antarctica. These winds are over 100 km per hour or like a cyclone in Australia.

The air is super cold, so no water is present. The rain falls as ice crystals.

Whiteout is a major issue in Antarctica. Whiteout is when the strong winds and loose snow blow so you cannot see anything.

People at these bases go outside for a moment and can get lost. They cannot find their way back to the cabin or base. The only thing they can see is a white wall of wind with snow crystals. They get lost and wander around until they freeze and die. If they go outside to look at something, they tie a rope to themselves that unwinds so they do not get lost.

5. Exploring the Coast

The area to explore is vast. If you look at the map, you can see Antarctica is bigger than Australia. It is a long way to walk to the South Pole. Walking there from Mawson's starting point was almost as far as walking across Australia. After they reached the South Pole, they still needed to trek back! The conditions would be incredibly cold and windy. Mawson wanted to explore an area below Australia. No-one had been there before, and Mawson wanted to gain information on this area. Mawson was part of a three-sled group who headed east in November 1912. Mawson, Ninnis and Mertz were one team.

South Sandwich
Islands (U.K.)

South Georgia
(U.K.)

SOUTH ATLANTIC OCEAN

South Orkney
Islands Orcadas (ARGENTINA)

Neumayer
(GERMANY)

Maitri   Novo-
SANAE IV (INDIA) lazarevskaya
(SOUTH AFRICA)   (RUSSIA)

Syowa (JAPAN)
Molodezhnaya
(RUSSIA)

Bernardo O'Higgins (CHILE) Esperanza (ARGENTINA)
Arturo Prat (CHILE) Marambio (ARGENTINA)

Queen Maud Land

Enderby
Land

Palmer (U.S.)
Vernadsky (UKRAINE)

Halley (U.K.)

Mawson (AUSTRALIA)

X

Weddell Sea

Rothera (U.K.) San Martin
(ARGENTINA)

Belgrano II (ARGENTINA)

Mac. Robertson
Land

Larsen Ice Shelf

Amery Ice Shelf

Alexander Island

Berkner Island

Zhong Shan (C)
Progress (RUSSIA)

Davis
(AUSTRALIA)

Ronne
Ice Shelf

Palmer
Land

Antarctica

X

Bellingshausen Sea

Peter Island

Ellsworth
Land

Amundsen-Scott (U.S.)

South Pole

Mirnyy (RUSSIA)

Shackleton
Ice Shelf

Vostok (RUSSIA)

SOUTH

Amundsen Sea

Marie Byrd
Land

Wilkes Land

Concordia
(FRANCE and ITALY)

Casey
(AUSTR.)

Ross
Ice Shelf

PACIFIC

McMurdo (U.S.)

INDIAN OCEAN

Scott (N.Z.)

Ross Sea

OCEAN

Victoria
Land

Dumont d'Urville
(FRANCE)

South Magnetic
Pole

Scott Island

Balleny
Islands

500   1000 km

500   1000 mi

Ninnis crossed a snow bridge. He did not know it was a crack in the ice. This crack in the ice is called a crevasse. The dog sled was crossing the snow bridge when it broke. The sled, dogs and explorer Ninnis fell into a deep break in the ice.

Mawson and Moritz looked for Ninnis but could not see him or hear him. They could see the sled and two of the dogs but not Ninnis. They waited all day and tried to climb down but did not have long ropes. Most of the food, equipment and tents had also fallen into the crevasse. They had only one week's food left.

They had to eat the sled dogs to stay alive. Moritz had eaten dog liver and it made him very ill. Moritz died in the night from liver poisoning. Mawson was now alone and still a long way from the hut.

Mawson had frost bite from his skin being frozen. This left large pieces of his face without skin. He nearly fell down a crevasse and was saved by his sled. By the time he got back to the hut, he was nearly dying. He was too late for the rescue ship.

35

Mawson had missed the supply ship only by a few hours. The other team had waited for him. They sent a wireless message to the ship but it was stuck in bad weather. If the supply ship had stayed it would have been stuck in the ice and crushed, so it had to leave. Mawson had to spend the whole winter again at Commonwealth Bay. The supply ship returned in December, 1913.

Antarctica is an open continent to all countries. Australia has made a claim to over 30% of the land but does not want it as a country. Australia shares this area with teams from China, Russia, and elsewhere. These teams are in Antarctica for research.

Antarctica is free from mines, factories and agriculture. The continent is not owned by any nation, and is protected from being damaged. It is very much hoped it stays that way.

6. Mawson's Achievements

The main purpose of all Mawson's work was science. The information on the rocks in Antarctica meant that more was known about the Earth and how it formed.

The group had explored large areas of Antarctica and written over 13 large science books on Antarctica.

Mawson went back to Australia and became a professor of geology at the University of Adelaide. He continued to write and be active about Antarctica for his whole life.

The study of Antarctic weather means we can understand how Australia's weather is formed. What we know about Antarctica today began with Mawson's team of explorers.

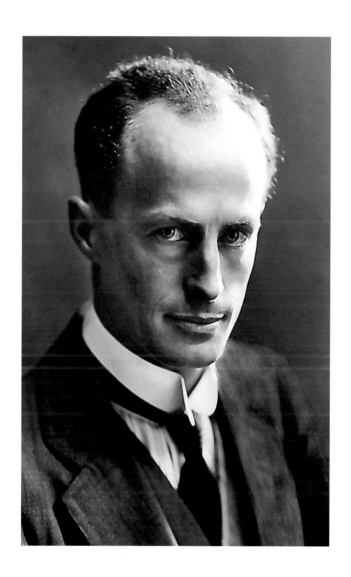

Mawson lived in Adelaide and was a professor for a long time. He died at the age of 76 years. He is remembered for his science and hard work to know more about Antarctica.

The trip across the ice was a terrible tragedy. Two men died and Mawson barely lived. It was not hero stuff but survival.

Mawson was there to study and not to be a legend. His coastal charting of the coast was superb and helped people know a lot more about Antarctica.

Word Bank

Antarctica	Aurora
geology	Australis
university	radiation
Adelaide	cyclone
continent	weather
Australia	temperature
America	glaciers
Mawson	linseed
happened	Commonwealth
exploring	expedition
important	crevasse
disappearing	poison
algae	kilometres
horizon	rescue
chocolate	information
everyone	understanding
beautiful	